3/11

J951 J

China in our world /

Sasl
S

COUNTRIES IN OUR WORLD

CHINA
IN OUR WORLD

Oliver James

A⁺
Smart Apple Media

Published by Smart Apple Media
P.O. Box 3263, Mankato, Minnesota 56002

Printed in the United States of America by Corporate
Graphics, North Mankato, Minnesota.

Published by arrangement with the Watts Publishing
Group Ltd., London.

Library of Congress Cataloging-in-Publication Data

James, Oliver, 1973-
  China in our world / by Oliver James.
      p. cm. -- (Countries in our world)
  Includes index.
  Summary: "Describes the economy, government, and
culture of China today and discusses China's influence
of and relations with the rest of the world"--Provided
by publisher.
  ISBN 978-1-59920-440-6 (library blinding)
  1. China--Juvenile literature. I. Title.
  DS706.J353 2011
  951.06--dc22

                                      2009031771

Produced by: White-Thomson Publishing Ltd.

Series consultant: Rob Bowden
Editor: Sonya Newland
Designer: Hayley Cove
Picture researcher: Rob Bowden

Picture Credits
Corbis: 8 (Chen Fei/Xinhua Press), 9 (China
Newsphoto/ Reuters), 15 (Lynsey Addario), 19 (Xu
Yu/Xinhua Press), 21 (Xiaoyang Liu), 26 (epa). **EASI-
Images:** Adrian Cooper 4, 12, 13, 14, 16, 18, 20, 24,
27, 29 / Tony Binns 6, 17, 22, 23 / Rob Bowden 7.
Photoshot: 10 (CNImaging). **Shutterstock:** 11 (Holger
Mette), 25 (Sam DCruz), 28 (rodho).

1207
32010

9 8 7 6 5 4 3 2 1

Contents

Introducing China

China is the fourth biggest country in the world, and it has the largest population. In 2008, almost one in every five people on Earth lived in China. For much of the last century, China was quite isolated, and had little impact on the rest of the world. This began to change in the 1970s, and China is now one of the most important and powerful countries in the world.

▼ Shanghai has always been a global city. It is now leading the rest of China toward becoming one of the world's superpowers.

▲ *China, along with Russia, has 14 international land borders—more than any other country in the world.*

A New World Power

In 2007, China became the fourth richest country in the world. It is now richer than the United Kingdom and France, and only Germany, Japan, and the United States are wealthier. China has some of the world's biggest companies, and its factories produce goods for export across the globe. In fact, China is so successful that you are probably wearing something made in China right now, or you will almost certainly use something made in China during your day.

Faster and Faster

As well as having a new global importance, there have also been great changes within China itself. The size of its cities, the number of cars on its roads, and the wealth of its people are all growing faster than in almost any other country in the world. Since 2000, China's economy grew three to four times faster than that of the United States or the United Kingdom. This growth began to slow down dramatically in 2008, though, as an economic crisis hit countries all over the world.

▲ *This man is making paper in the same way that it was made in China over 2,000 years ago.*

IT STARTED HERE

Paper

The Chinese first invented paper-making around 2,200 years ago. It was commonly used for writing around 1,700 years ago. By about 1,500 years ago, it was even being used as toilet paper!

China in Need

China's growth has been so rapid that it cannot meet all its own needs. It does not have enough of many basic resources, such as lumber and steel, which are needed for building or as raw materials for industry, so it must import these items from other countries. China is one of the world's biggest consumers of resources. In 2006, it was estimated that half of all the trees cut down in the world were used by China. And in 2008, China used nearly one-third of all the steel produced in the world.

China and the World

Today, China has a major influence on the rest of the world—its use of steel, for example, has led to shortages in other countries. However, China has been influencing the world for hundreds, even thousands of years. Many things we use or enjoy originally came from China, including fireworks, kite flying, silk, pasta, umbrellas, paper money, and the compass.

BASIC DATA

Official name: **People's Republic of China**

Capital: **Beijing**

Size: **3,705,407 sq miles (9,596,960 sq km)**

Population: **1,338,612,968 (2009 est.)**

Currency: **Yuan (¥)**

Chinese Around the World

Another way that China influences the world is in the spread of its people. Chinese communities can now be found across the globe, and the Chinese people have taken their customs and culture with them. Chinese food, for example, is now one of the world's most popular foods.

▼ *A dragon-dance team takes part in a Chinese New Year celebration in Sydney, Australia. Sydney has a large Chinese population.*

Landscapes and Environment

China is so large that each area of the country has a different landscape and environment. In the north and west, China is high and dry, but in the south and east, it is lower and wetter. China's mountains, rivers, deserts, and coasts are among the largest on Earth.

PLACE IN THE WORLD

Total area: **3,705,407 sq miles (9,596,960 sq km)**

Percentage of world land area: **6.4%**

World ranking: **4th**

The Roof of the World

The highest part of China is the Tibetan Plateau. It covers an enormous area of land—almost four times bigger than Texas. Most of the Plateau is over 13,100 to 16,400 ft (4,000 to 5,000 m) above sea level. This is about as tall as Mr. Elbert, the highest peak of the Rocky Mountains in the U.S. The Plateau is very cold for most of the year, and few people live there. Lhasa is the main city in the region.

▼ *A lama (monk) walks across Potala Palace square in Lhasa, the capital of Tibet and the main settlement on the vast Tibetan Plateau.*

▲ *Visitors watch the Hukou Waterfall on the Yellow River. The color—and the river's name—comes from sediment in the water.*

IT'S A FACT!

Mount Everest, which lies on the border between China and Nepal, is the world's highest mountain, at 29,035 ft (8,850 m) above sea level. China also shares the world's second highest mountain with Pakistan. It is called K2 and stands 28,251 ft (8,611 m) above sea level.

Rivers of China

China's most important river, the Yangtze— or Chang Jiang as it is called in China—begins on the Tibetan Plateau. From there, it crosses the country and joins the East China Sea near Shanghai. At 3,915 miles (6,300 km), it is the third longest river in the world. It is important for transport and trade, and the land around the river produces nearly half of China's crops. Nearly one-third of China's people live along its path. The Yellow River (Huang He) is China's other main river, and is 3,395 miles (5,464 km) long. It also starts on the Tibetan Plateau and flows across northern China to the Yellow Sea.

9

Deserts of the North

China has two major deserts. The Gobi Desert lies along the border with Mongolia and is a mostly rocky desert. It has been growing since the 1950s and is now less than 50 miles (80 km) from Beijing. The Takla Makan Desert is in northwest China and is about the size of Arizona. It is one of the largest sandy deserts in the world: in some places the sand is 1,000 ft (300 m) deep! No one lives in the Takla Makan Desert because strong winds there cause sand storms almost every day of the year.

◀ *A man wades through Zhangzhou city in June 2008 after storms led to localized flooding. An early warning system meant that few people were harmed, but many properties were damaged.*

Natural Hazards

Flooding has killed millions of people in China over the last 150 years, especially on the Yellow and Yangtze Rivers. Tropical storms can damage settlements along the coast, but early warning systems and shelters mean that few people are killed. Earthquakes are much harder to predict. In 2008, a major earthquake hit Sichuan province in the center of China, killing 70,000 people and making more than four million homeless.

IT'S A FACT!

The Yellow River is known in China as the "river of sorrow" because it has the record for the worst floods of all time. In 1887, the river burst its banks and killed up to 2.5 million people. It flooded again in 1931, killing an estimated one to two million people, making it easily the deadliest river in the world.

Endangered Wildlife

China's fast growth has harmed many natural environments. Rivers and forests have been especially damaged by industry, farming, and transport. Pandas have lost large areas of their natural bamboo forests, and the rare Yangtze River dolphin may already be extinct. Scientists could not find a single one after searching for six weeks in 2007.

▼ *The giant panda is one of China's most endangered species, and has become a symbol of conservation work worldwide. These pandas are at a breeding center in Chengdu.*

GLOBAL LEADER

Hydroelectric Power (HEP)

China's Three Gorges Dam across the Yangtze River is the world's biggest HEP dam. When it is finished in 2011, it will produce the same amount of electricity as 15 coal-powered plants. However, the lake created by the dam will force thousands of people to leave their homes, and there are also concerns about the impact the dam will have on local wildlife.

Population and Migration

China has more people living in it than any other country. In fact, if the global population was just 100 people, then 20 of them would be from China. This is compared to 17 from India, 4.5 from the United States, and less than one from the United Kingdom.

PLACE IN THE WORLD

Population: **1,338,612,968**

Percentage of world total: **19.9%**

World ranking: **1st**

Growing Fast

In 1900, China had around 430 million people, but this increased to 555 million by 1950. In the second half of the twentieth century, improvements in health care helped the population grow even faster. By 1981, it had passed one billion, and by 2000, China had an amazing 1.26 billion people. This means that between 1950 and 2000, China's population increased by about 27 people every minute! It has slowed down since then, but is still growing by around 16 people per minute.

▶ *China is constantly building to keep pace with its enormous and fast growing population.*

Too Many People

When a population grows quickly, it can be difficult to keep up with the need for food, water, housing, health care, and education. In 1979, China decided to solve this problem by limiting each family to just one child. These one-child families would be well cared for by the government. However, if people chose to have larger families, they would be fined or could even lose their jobs.

The One-Child Policy

By 2008, China said that its one-child policy had reduced population growth by at least 300 million people. This is about the same as the entire population of the United States! One problem with the policy is that there are now around 117 boys for every 100 girls in China. Parents would rather have a boy, and many have chosen not to keep the baby if they find out it is a girl.

GOING GLOBAL

China has one of the largest overseas populations of any country. Between 35 and 60 million Chinese people live outside China, mostly in other Asian countries or in North America and Europe. The United States has around three million Chinese and Canada has over one million.

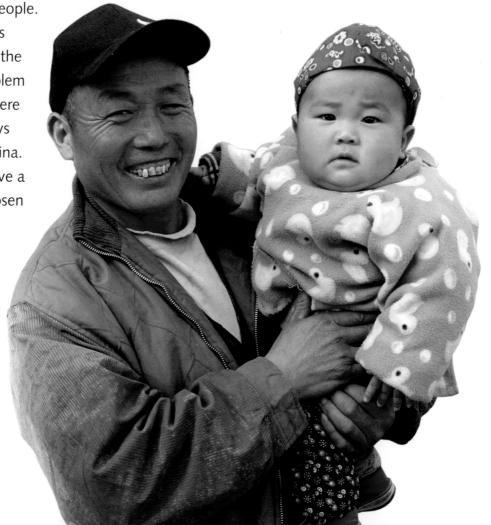

▶ *A grandfather stands with his granddaughter. It is common in China for grandparents to care for children while their parents are out working.*

China's Growing Cities

In 1950, most Chinese people lived in rural areas, and only 13 in every 100 people lived in towns or cities. Since then, China's urban areas have grown very quickly, and by 2008 they were home to around 43 percent of the population. China has some of the largest cities in the world. Shanghai has around 15.5 million people, and Beijing around 11.5 million. In total, China has 109 cities with a population of more than one million, compared to 42 in the United States and only six in Canada.

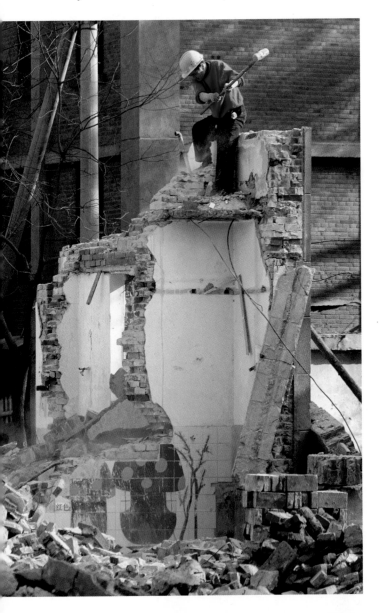

Leaving China

Every year, an estimated one to two million people leave China in search of work. They follow others, and there are now Chinese communities in more than 140 countries. In many places, Chinese migrants choose to live together in one community. They have their own restaurants and shops specializing in Chinese food and other goods. In cities such as New York, London, and Sydney, these areas are known as "Chinatown."

◀ *As China's cities grow, many older structures are being demolished to make way for new and bigger buildings to house even more people.*

IT'S A FACT!

The number of people living in China's towns and cities is almost double the entire population of the United States, or nearly 40 times the population of Canada!

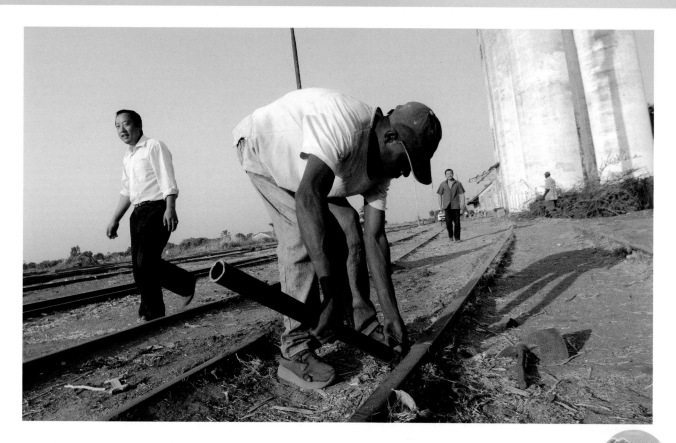

▲ *Chinese workers oversee the construction of a new railway in Angola, Africa. Chinese laborers are involved in similar projects around the world.*

Overseas Labor

China has many skilled workers who can offer expertise to other countries at a low cost. Chinese companies and workers have become global leaders in large construction projects, for example. In Africa, they have built many roads, railroads, dams, and bridges. In the Caribbean, they have built government offices and sports stadiums, such as the new Antigua and Barbuda stadium, which was built for the 2007 Cricket World Cup.

GLOBAL LEADER

Dongtan Eco-city

By 2010, China hopes to open the world's first environmentally friendly city, on an island in the Yangtze River. Dongtan Eco-city will provide homes and work for around 10,000 people. Energy will come from the wind, sun, biofuels, and recycled waste. Public transportation will use clean fuels, and people will be encouraged to ride bicycles and walk. Farms will produce organic food for the city and take away waste for turning into compost.

Over the centuries, China's ancient and fascinating culture has spread all around the world. It was also closely linked to the way Chinese people lived. This is changing now, though, as China is having to balance traditions with new ideas and influences coming from other parts of the world.

Religion and Beliefs

China has been an important center of religious beliefs for hundreds of years. Confucianism and Daoism (Taoism) are especially important, and had a big influence on Chinese rulers. In the twentieth century, religion was restricted because the government believed it threatened its control. People now have greater religious freedom, but some beliefs, such as Falun Gong, are still banned. The main religions in China are Confucianism, Daoism, and Buddhism, with a smaller number following Islam or Christianity. About 40 percent of Chinese say they have no religion at all.

FAMOUS CHINESE

Confucius (551–479 BC)

Confucius was a great thinker who believed that learning allowed all people to improve themselves and their communities. His thoughts were the basis of Chinese society for around 2,000 years.

▶ *Confucius is one of China's most important historical figures. His ideas about how we should live have influenced people around the world.*

▲ *Villagers bathe their buffalo in front of their rice paddies. This is typical of many rural villages, where life has changed little in hundreds of years.*

Growing Up in China

A child growing up in one of China's cities will have a very different life from a child growing up in rural China. In cities, most people live in apartment blocks, but in rural areas families live in simple one-story, two-room houses with animals grazing outside. City life is made easier with technology, such as computers, and modern appliances, such as refrigerators and washing machines. In rural areas, people are less likely to have these, and instead have the basic equipment needed to grow crops and look after animals.

THE HOME OF...

Traditional Chinese Medicine

Traditional Chinese medicine has been practiced in China for over 3,000 years. Illnesses such as skin complaints, fevers, and throat infections are treated using mixtures of dried plant, mineral, and animal ingredients. Chinese medicine is now popular with non-Chinese people around the world as an alternative to Western drugs. Chinese medicine has been criticized for encouraging a trade in rare animals whose body parts are believed to have special properties. These include rhino horns and tiger bones.

Feeding the People

Food is an important part of cultural life in China, but feeding 1.3 billion people is also a major challenge. Rice is China's main food and has been grown there for over 8,000 years. Although modern rice-farming machinery has been introduced, many small farms still use animal power and farm rice by hand. China exports only around 1 percent of its rice, but it produces so much that it is still the world's sixth largest exporter.

IT STARTED HERE

Pasta

Pasta is often thought of as Italian, but a 4,000-year-old bowl of noodles found in China shows that the Chinese were probably the first to invent pasta making.

◀ *Street food, such as that served at this chow mein stall, is popular. More unusual offerings include deep fried scorpions or grasshoppers!*

Changing Diets

As people become richer and new tastes arrive from outside the country, Chinese diets are changing. Traditionally, most people would eat either rice or noodles with vegetables, with small amounts of meat or fish as a side dish. A more Western style diet, with more meat, fish, and dairy products, and higher levels of fat and sugar, is now common in China. This has made the Chinese people overweight, too. Since 1990, the number of overweight or obese people has almost tripled to around 325 million in 2008.

Health and Sports

Personal fitness is important to Chinese people. In large cities across the country, people gather each morning to practice a traditional type of exercise and martial art called tai chi chuan. Other martial arts, including judo and karate, are also popular. Badminton, diving, and table tennis are among China's most successful sports. Imported sports, such as soccer and basketball, have become popular, too.

THE HOME OF...

Chinese Astrology

Chinese astrology follows a 12-year cycle, with each year named after its own animal. Astrologers believe that someone's personality depends on which animal sign they were born under. The 12 animals are: rat, tiger, dragon, horse, monkey, dog, ox, rabbit, snake, sheep, rooster, and pig.

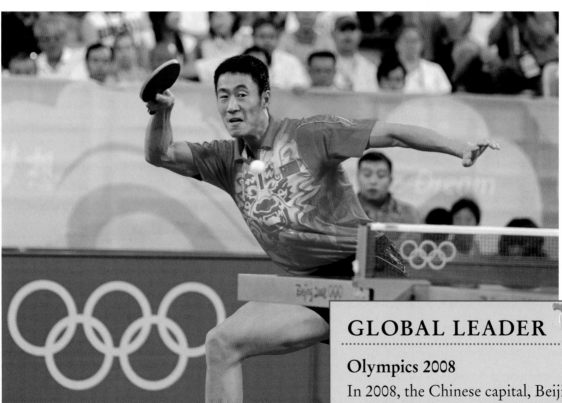

▲ *Wang Liqin won a gold medal in table tennis at the 2008 Olympics in Beijing. Table tennis is one of the most popular sports in China.*

GLOBAL LEADER

Olympics 2008

In 2008, the Chinese capital, Beijing, hosted the 29th Olympic Games. The Chinese team won more gold medals than any other nation, taking 51 of the 302 gold medals awarded.

Economy and Trade

China's economy has grown so quickly that it has often been called an economic miracle. In the 1960s, China had very little international trade, but today goods made in China are sold in almost every corner of the world.

◀ Women working in the service sector— in a shop that sells CDs and DVDs. China now produces such items for the global market.

Open for Business

In 1978, the Chinese government decided to open the economy to greater trade with other countries. They set up special areas where foreign companies could build factories and where goods could be imported and exported. As trade increased, China's economy began to grow, and by 1990, the wealth of the country had almost doubled.

IT STARTED HERE

Paper Money

It is thought that paper money was first used in ancient China in around 800 AD. During a shortage of copper, the emperor at the time allowed paper bills to be issued in exchange for cash. Because they were lighter than coins, the idea caught on, and within 100 years paper money was used all over China. Early Chinese paper bills had coins printed on them to remind people who couldn't read what the bill was for!

It Just Keeps Growing

By 2008, the Chinese economy was 8.8 times bigger than it had been in 1990. By comparison, the world's biggest economy—the United States—grew by just 2.4 times in the same period. The world economy slowed in 2008, but in China, it is still predicted to grow at around 9 percent. This is mainly because of the country's lead role in global trade, with more and more goods being "made in China."

▼ *An excursion boat passes in front of Pudong in Shanghai, China's main financial district, and a global symbol of China's rapid economic growth.*

Changing Economy

As China's economy has grown, its structure has also changed. In 1990, agriculture was responsible for about 27 percent of China's economy, but by 2007 this had fallen to just 11 percent. As farming has decreased in importance for the economy, industry and manufacturing have increased. They made up almost half of the economy in 2007. The other growing area is services, which include trade, transportation, retail, and other areas such as banking, insurance, health care, and education. These now make up around 40 percent of the economy.

▲ *Farming is still labor intensive in many parts of China, especially at key times such as harvest. These people are separating wheat grain from the waste after it has been harvested.*

Work, Work, Work

Chinese people are extremely hard working, but this is sometimes abused by companies that make people work long hours for low wages. Long working hours are also blamed for the high number of accidents at Chinese factories, mines, and building sites. Farming is still the biggest employer in China, but more and more people are leaving to try to find factory or office jobs in the cities. Some will even leave China to find work and send money home to their families. In 2007, Chinese workers living overseas sent US$25.7 billion back home to their families—more than any other country except India.

IT'S A FACT!

China has the world's biggest workforce, with over 800 million people in 2007. This is greater than the entire population of the United States and the European Union combined!

Trade, Trade, Trade

The import and export of goods and services made up nearly three-quarters of China's economy in 2007. Its main exports are manufactured goods, such as toys, electronic items, tools, and textiles. It is estimated that Chinese factories make around 50 percent of the world's computers, 60 percent of its digital cameras, and 65 percent of all cell phones!

Most of these are made in China for foreign companies, but Chinese companies are now growing, too. By 2008, there were more than 5,000 Chinese companies with business investments in 172 countries and regions around the world.

PLACE IN THE WORLD

Gross Domestic Product (GDP):
US$4.222 trillion (2008 est.)

Percentage of world total: 6.7%

World ranking: 3rd

▼ *Tourism is one of China's fastest-growing trades. In 2007, 55 million visitors spent US$42 billion. The Great Wall of China is the most popular tourist attraction.*

Buying the World

China's enormous population and growing economy is very demanding. The construction of new buildings, for example, means that China was using about 46 percent of the world's cement by 2006. The biggest concern, however, is over food. In early 2008, world food shortages and rising prices were blamed partly on China's growing demand for food. As incomes increase and diets change, this demand will increase even more. Some experts are worried that this could have a major impact on other countries, especially poorer ones without the economic power that China has.

Government and Politics

China has one of the oldest civilizations on Earth, but by the early twentieth century, its leadership was weak from years of war and conflict. In 1949, a new China emerged and was named the People's Republic of China. It was the start of communist rule in China, and began a period of incredible change that continues today.

FAMOUS CHINESE

Mao Zedong (1893–1976)

Mao Zedong is often called "the father of modern China." His leadership was not all good, though. In 1958, he introduced new farming plans that led to a massive famine that killed 20 million people.

Total Control

Communism is where the government has total control over the way a country is run. Where people live and work, what they learn and eat, and even when they can marry, are all decided by the government. China's first communist leader, Mao Zedong, introduced many controls when he came to power in 1954, and banned all opposition to the government. He was very suspicious of Western countries such as the United States and United Kingdom, so for many years China was cut off from the rest of the world.

▶ A portrait of Mao Zedong, China's most influential leader of recent times, hangs on the palace known as the Forbidden City in Beijing.

Land Arguments

Modern China includes areas of land that others say do not belong to China. The most famous is Tibet, which was occupied by the Chinese in 1950. In 1959, the spiritual leader of Tibet, the Dalai Lama, was forced to leave, and Tibet became an official region of China in 1965. Since then, many organizations have campaigned asking China to free Tibet and let the Tibetan people rule themselves once again. The Free Tibet movement is an international campaign that has supporters all over the world.

▲ *These people in Vancouver, Canada, are protesting against the Chinese occupation of Tibet.*

IT'S A FACT!

The Chinese government employs more than 10 million officials. This is far more than in any other country, and is greater than the population of many countries!

Looking Out

The death of Mao Zedong in 1976 marked a change in China's relationship with the world. By 1978, China had agreed a new political friendship with the U.S., and agreements with other countries soon followed. China's main reason for building such relationships is to help its own trade and industry.

▼ *China's President Hu Jintao (left) and his Sudanese counterpart Omar Hassan al-Bashir (right) shake hands at a meeting in Sudan, at which China promised greater links with Sudan.*

China and Africa

Since 2000, China has been building new political friendships with Africa. African countries have large reserves of energy and other resources that China needs. In return for supplies of oil, copper, and other resources, China is giving African leaders billions of dollars in aid. Although this is good for China, the country has been criticized for giving aid to countries where there is war or conflict. This is because of fears that the money is being used for fighting instead of development in countries such as Sudan and Zimbabwe.

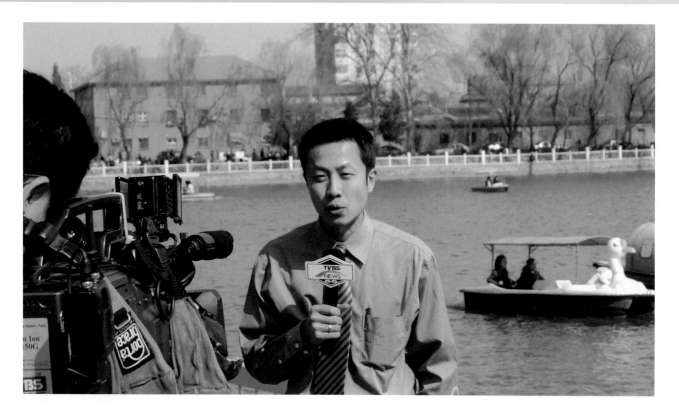

Human Rights

China may have opened up to the world, but it is still very strict with its own people. Criminals in China can be executed for crimes such as stealing gasoline or avoiding taxes, for example. The Chinese government also controls media, such as newspapers and television, and it decides which web sites the Chinese people can access. Some people believe that this is a violation of human and civil rights.

▲ *A Chinese news reporter filming on location in Beijing. The government is criticized for its strict control over the media.*

GOING GLOBAL

In 2006, trade between Africa and China was worth around US$30 billion—six times more than in 2000. By 2010, it is expected to increase to over US$100 billion.

Global Superpower

China is one of only five permanent members of the United Nations (UN) Security Council. This is the most important part of the UN and is responsible for keeping global peace. This gives China great power in world affairs, but its growing economic wealth makes it even more powerful. Some experts believe that China could soon pass the U.S. to become the most powerful country in the world.

Since China began to open up to the world in 1978, its economy has grown by around 9.5 percent every year. Few other countries can match this, but what will China do in the future? Some believe it has grown too fast and will collapse, but others see no end to China's incredible success.

▼ *A new luxury housing development in southeast China. These houses are aimed at China's new rich as homes or vacation homes.*

Business as Usual

If China's economy continues to grow as it has since 1978, it is likely that by 2020 it will have passed the United States as the world's richest country. It will have passed Japan and Germany by 2015. But not everything will be easy for China. Its population will have grown to around 1.42 billion and 53 percent of them (756 million) will live in towns and cities. China will need several cities like Dongtan (see page 15) if it is to support this increase without destroying its already delicate environment.

▲ *Fashion is becoming increasingly popular in China as the wealth of the country continues to rise.*

Future Changes

Although China has been catching up to Western countries, it will need to find new ways to develop in the future. Using more renewable energy will reduce its impact on the environment and limit pollution. The government may also need to rethink the one-child policy, as there are concerns that China will not have enough young people to care for its aging population. At the moment there is only one child for every two parents and four grandparents!

China in the World

If everyone in China chose to live in the same way as an average American or European by the year 2020, then it would have a major impact on the world. Changes in diet would mean a shortage of food, and greater energy use would lead to global fuel shortages. But China and its people have a right to develop. The solution is for China— and all countries—to make lifestyle choices that allow everyone to benefit more equally in the future.

Glossary

astrology the study of the influence of the stars, planets, sun, and moon on human affairs.

biofuels fuels that come from recently dead materials, usually plants, instead of fossil fuels, such as coal.

Buddhism a religion that follows the teachings of Buddha (*c.* 563-483 BC), and involves studying wisdom, meditation, and following an ethical code.

Christianity a religion that follows the teachings of Jesus Christ.

Confucianism a philosophy or way of life based around the teachings of Confucius (551-479 BC).

conservation looking after the natural environment and wildlife.

Daoism a system of philosophical beliefs that focuses on an ethical code and encourages compassion toward others.

economy the financial system of a country or region, including how much money is made from the production and sale of goods and services.

export to send or transport products or materials abroad for sale or trade.

Falun Gong a spiritual movement that began in China in the late twentieth century, based on Buddhist and Daoist teachings and practices.

GDP (Gross Domestic Product) the value of all goods and services produced by a country in a year.

human rights the basic rights and freedoms to which all humans are entitled, such as the right to food, shelter, education, and protection by the law.

hydroelectric power electricity that is generated using the energy from running water.

import to bring in goods or materials from a foreign country for sale.

Islam a religion with belief in one god (Allah) and his last prophet, Muhammad.

martial arts the Asian arts of combat (fighting) or self-defense, such as karate, judo, and aikido.

migrants people who move from one place to another to live or work.

organic made only from animal or vegetable materials, without any chemical substances.

raw materials unprocessed natural products, such as iron ore or coal.

resources things that are available to use, often to help develop a country's industry and economy. Resources could be minerals, workers (labor), or water.

textiles cloth or fabric, usually made from weaving.

Further Information

Books

China
Changing World
by Jen Green
(Arcturus Publishing, 2009)

China Focus: Changing China
by Marta Segal Block
(Heinemann Library, 2008)

China
Countries in the News
by Iris Techmann
(Smart Apple Media, 2008)

China
World in Focus
by Ali Brownlie Bojang
(World Almanac Library, 2006)

Looking at China
Looking at Countries
by Jillian Powell
(Gareth Stevens Publishing, 2008)

Teens in China
Global Connections
by Karen Elizabeth Conyers
(Compass Point Books, 2007)

Web Sites

http://www.chinadaily.com.cn
China's English-language newspaper online.

http://china.org.cn
General information about China.

http://www.cyberschoolbus.un.org/infonation/index.asp
United Nations web site information about all countries for children.

https://www.cia.gov/library/publications/the-world-factbook/geos/ch.html
CIA World Factbook on China.

Every effort has been made by the publisher to ensure that these web sites contain no inappropriate or offensive material. However, because of the nature of the Internet, it is impossible to guarantee that the contents of these sites will not be altered. We strongly advise that Internet access is supervised by a responsible adult.

Index

Numbers in **bold** indicate pictures